In Search of the
Little Count
Joseph Boruwlaski,
Durham Celebrity

by

Simon Webb

Published by the Langley Press

© 2018 Simon Webb. The right of Simon Webb to be identified as the Author of the Work has been asserted by him in accordance with the Copyright, Designs and Patents Act 1988. All rights reserved.

Dedicated to those of us who are not exactly Johnny Weissmuller.

Cover picture reproduced with kind permission from Durham County Council, as are other pictures marked DCC. Pictures marked WM are public domain images from Wikimedia Commons.

Also from the Langley Press

Victorian Durham

The Founding of Durham

The Bishopric of Durham

The Dunbar Martyrs: Scottish prisoners of War in Durham Cathedral, 1650

Plain Tales from the Durham Light Infantry

The Book of Esau:
A Murder Mystery of Victorian Durham

Mary Ann Cotton: Victorian Serial Killer

For free downloads and more from the Langley Press, please visit our website at:

http://tinyurl.com/lpdirect

Contents

1. The Count's House	5
2. The Little Person	10
3. Friend Of The Rich And Famous	15
4. The Wandering Minstrel	31
5. Little Poland	62
6. Epilogue In Narnia	77
Further Reading	79

1. The Count's House

When autumn comes to Durham, and a papery mist settles on the river, it is easy to see why this northern English city has spawned so many legends.

There is the legend of the foundation of the city, when a party of monks carrying the coffin of St Cuthbert were summoned by a vision to this wild, wooded place, which they hadn't even heard of before. There is also the legend of a writer called C.S. Lewis who, pausing under a lamp-post by the river, dreamed up a series of novels which would ignite the imaginations of children round the world for decades. And finally there is the legend of the tiny Pole who found his long longed-for sanctuary in the city, and his final resting-place in its great church.

The most ancient part of the city of Durham is built on a huge, flat-topped rock, which is embraced by a loop of the river Wear. If you walk around the inner banks of the river at Durham you will eventually come across a mysterious stone temple that would not look out of place among the ruins of the Acropolis in Athens.

The Durham people call this part of the river the Count's Corner, and they call the building the Count's House, in memory of a Polish aristocrat who once lived in the city. That an exotic East-European toff should have lived at Durham is interesting in itself, but Joseph Boruwlaski was no ordinary Polish count. He was a guitarist, a traveller, an alchemist, a health nut, an outrageous flirt and a close friend of the famous Georgiana, Duchess of Devonshire. He was also a record-breaker – a tiny little person who lived to be nearly one hundred years old. (The phrases 'little person' and 'little people' are used here in place of 'dwarf' and 'dwarfs', except in inverted commas, or where the job-description of 'court dwarf' is meant.)

The exact link between Joseph Boruwlaski and the so-called Count's House is a matter of debate. Some say there is no real link, and that the local people, seeing what looks like a little house, and knowing that a famous little person had once lived nearby, assumed that the Count had lived there.

They would have been quite wrong to assume this: it is unlikely that anyone ever lived in the Count's House on a permanent basis. The place is obviously quite unsuited to human habitation, especially during the cold northern winters. There is no door, and the large windows never seem to have had glass in them. There is no sign of any kind of heating system, or running water, or other mod cons. Until metal grilles were installed over the door and windows, some rough-sleepers sheltered there, but the Count's House is not really a house at all. Even if it had been fitted up as a house years ago, it is surely too small for even a little person to have lived there, especially with the two women who lived with him.

The second theory about the Count's House is that, when the Count's real house was demolished, the portico was salvaged and the rest of the little temple built onto it. The problem with this theory is that a surviving picture of the Count's actual residence in Durham shows a very plain little cottage with no portico – at least not around the front door. It is possible that Joseph had a portico added to the back entrance, but it would have looked rather out of place. We must also remember that this house was not really his, but had been rented to him by the dean and chapter. People are far less likely to improve a house that is not their property than they are to embellish a building that actually belongs to them.

The third theory about the stone temple is that it was erected as a memorial to the Count after his death. This too seems unlikely. The Count had already left a lasting memorial to himself in the form of the various editions, in both French and English, of his autobiography. There are also drawings, engravings, oil-paintings, a statue; and a stone plaque inside the Church of St Mary the Less in Durham. The Count's burial-place under the flagstones of Durham Cathedral is also marked with a stone bearing his initials.

There is, furthermore, no sign of any dedicatory inscription to Boruwlaski anywhere on the temple. A temple would, in any case, be a very unusual monument if built to commemorate the life of a person. In England, people who are felt to deserve more than just a headstone are usually commemorated with plaques, statues or reliefs, either on or near a tomb, or in some public place.

A fourth theory as to the origins of the temple is that it was used as a sort of ornate shed by Boruwlaski's gardener. This idea is easily knocked on the head, as no self-respecting gardener would keep so much as a broken spade in a building without a door or windows; and an 1820 map of the area shows various other small buildings nearby that could have been sheds or green-houses.

The last theory as to the link between the little temple and the Count states that the building was once a sort of picturesque folly in Boruwlaski's garden. This seems the most likely explanation. The temple is in roughly the right place to have stood at the eastern end of the Count's land, as shown in the 1820 map. The old map doesn't show the temple itself, which suggests that it was erected later. This is consistent with the style of the temple: in his book on Durham buildings, Nikolaus Pevsner suggests that it was built in the 1820s or 30s.

The architectural style of the building is also consistent with its having been designed for, or even by, a Polish count. The Poles have long had a fondness for classical architecture in the Greek and Roman style, and many buildings in both Krakow and Warsaw feature Doric, Ionic and Corinthian columns, with doors and windows arranged in classic fashion.

In fact the Count's old friend and patron, King Stanislaw II of Poland, was particularly energetic about building, for instance, customs-houses that looked like Greek temples.

The Count's House is located on what would have been the part of Boruwlaski's land with the best view of the river. This is another significant detail: it is clear from his autobiographies that the Count was fascinated by bodies of water of any kind, ranging from the sea right down to tiny streams. He seems to have found it impossible to describe any place, even a house, without giving special attention to any nearby water-features. He was also a devotee of fresh air, and the breeze from the river in this part of Durham can be decidedly fresh, even in summer.

It is easy to imagine how the Count might have used this building. He would have entertained his friends here during clement weather, and even given recitals on the violin or guitar. The temple might also have acted as a solitary refuge for the Count, perhaps on days when his servant was cleaning, or when the Misses Ebdon, with whom he lived, were receiving visitors he didn't want to meet. One can imagine him sitting there reading some calf-covered volume from his collection of books, occasionally referring to his fine gold watch to check if it was safe to return to the cottage.

2. The Little Person

Jozef Boruwlaski was not a count by birth - his title was supposedly conferred on him later by King Stanislaw II of Poland. After he settled in England, he Anglicised the spelling of his name to 'Joseph Boruwlaski'.

People often got the spelling wrong, both before and after Joseph modified it. The author who put Joseph into the French *Encyclopedie* called him 'Borwilaski'. The 1820 map tells us his land is occupied by 'Count Borowloskie', and even Pevsner rendered his surname as 'Boruwlawski'. The London *Times* called him 'Borawlaski', 'Borowlaski' and even 'Bouwlaski'.

If the spellings were varied, we can be sure that attempts by his English friends to pronounce his surname were even more diverse. Some Britons abandoned the attempt altogether and called Joseph 'Barrel-of-whisky' or 'Lord Tom Thumb'. The second of these nicknames was not a reference to Charles Stratton, or 'General Tom Thumb', the famous entertainer who worked for P.T. Barnum: Stratton was born the year after Boruwlaski died. The original Tom Thumb was a legendary little person who was supposed to have lived with King Arthur's knights at Camelot.

'Barrel-of-whisky' isn't far off the correct pronunciation of Joseph's surname, as in Polish 'w' is usually pronounced like an English 'v' and the crossed 'l' is pronounced like a 'w'.

Joseph was born near Halicz in Poland in 1739. This date is an especially valuable one, since his various autobiographies contain few reliable dates, and the events presented in them sometimes seem to be in the wrong order.

Some events happen at times when they couldn't have happened, and some events really couldn't have happened at all. In this book, I have tried to concentrate on the more likely events.

1739, the year of Joseph's birth, saw Britain beginning the notorious War of Jenkin's Ear against Spain, and it also saw the death of the semi-legendary highwayman, Dick Turpin. His 1739 birth made Boruwlaski a year older than the Marquis de Sade, Beethoven's father, and James Boswell (biographer of Samuel Johnson).

The Poland Boruwlaski was born in was the Polish-Lithuanian Commonwealth, a huge country, bigger than Spain and Portugal put together. His father was a member of the Polish nobility, but the family had little money or property. Boruwlaski's father had been a supporter of the ill-fated Polish King Stanislaw I. Stanislaw had been crowned King of Poland twice, but had also lost his kingdom twice and ended up as the ruler of some estates in France. As a result of his loyalty to this unfortunate monarch, Boruwlaski's father lost his own estate near the Dneipr river and was forced to move west and live in reduced circumstances near the Dneistr, at Halicz (now in the modern state of Ukraine).

Joseph was one of six children, no less than three of whom were little people. He was only nine inches

(23 cm) long at birth. This is somewhat less than half the average length at birth of modern babies. In his autobiographies, he tells us he continued to grow until he was thirty years old, at which point he stopped at the height of three feet and three inches (99cm). Today, this is around the average height for a Caucasian boy of three and a half years. The average modern adult white man would stand about thirty-one inches (78cm) taller than the Little Count.

His friend the comedian Charles Mathews believed, however, that Joseph was still growing well into old age. The Count told Mathews that in five hundred years he would be as tall as Mathews himself; tall enough, in fact, to be a grenadier.

Given the small size of two of his siblings, it is pretty obvious that Boruwlaski's restricted growth was due to some genetic condition, but which condition? Margot Johnson, author of the *Dictionary of National Biography* article on Boruwlaski, insists that the cause of his smallness was achondroplasia. People with achondroplasia have trouble producing enough bone to grow to normal size. They tend to have large heads and torsos in comparison to their limbs, which appear unusually short, even at birth.

In contrast to Margot Johnson, Armand Marie Leroi, in his book *Mutants*, states that Joseph Boruwlaski was a little person because of a pituitary problem.

The pituitary is a pea-sized gland at the base of the brain, which surgeons can reach through the roof of the mouth. Its main job is to produce growth hormone. If this process is compromised in some way (for instance if the gland itself is unusually small) the result can be restricted growth.

Leroi justifies his pituitary diagnosis for the Count by pointing to the proportions of his body, which resembled those of a person of average size, except that his head was disproportionately large. Most adult humans, both male and female, tend to have bodies that are about seven and a half times taller than their own heads. Careful measurement of a photograph of the Count's statue reveals that his body was only six and a half times taller than his own head.

The statue, by T. Bonomi, may not have been made to the right proportions, but these proportions do broadly agree with those seen in two-dimensional likenesses of the Count.

Joseph doesn't seem to have had the proportionately short limbs of the typical person with achondroplasia, whose arms may not even stretch down to their hips. The fact that Boruwlaski was often mistaken for a child, even when he was quite old, would also seem to add weight to Leroi's theory.

Short of digging up the Count's bones, it is unlikely that the exact nature of his condition will ever be known for sure, especially since all the surviving likenesses of him are drawings, paintings and engravings; not forgetting the statue. If he had lived just a little longer, we might now have a photograph of him, which could have added more information to the debate about his condition. Unfortunately, Joseph Boruwlaski died in 1837, just two years before two different practical systems for photography were introduced, by Daguerre in France and Fox-Talbot in England.

It may be that even an examination of Boruwlaski's remains would not find evidence of any of the medical conditions that can restrict growth. Some people are just very short, for no particular reason.

Although Joseph's physical measurements were of course small, the length of his life was remarkably long. He lived to the age of ninety-eight.

In the twenty-first century it is becoming more commonplace for people to live into their nineties, even with what were once regarded as very serious medical conditions. This was by no means common in the late eighteenth and early nineteenth centuries. Even in 1841, three years after Boruwlaski died, the average life expectancy for boys at birth was only slightly over forty years. This statistic will have been dragged down by the tragically high numbers of infant mortalities, of course.

The extreme length of Joseph's life means that the biographer has to deal in decades rather than years, and the shortness of, and lack of detail in, the Count's autobiographies mean that long stretches of time are not accounted for. The last edition of Boruwlaski's autobiography was published in 1820, when the Count still had seventeen years to live.

As if both his mind and body somehow knew he would live a long time, Joseph took some aspects of his life rather slowly. He didn't reach puberty until quite late, and he himself admits that he was still acting like a teenager when he was in his mid-twenties. He also got married quite late in life.

3. Friend of the Rich And Famous

Boruwlaski's father died when Joseph was only nine, and the poverty- stricken state of the family became even more desperate. Luckily a wealthy friend of his mother, a noblewoman called the Starostin de Caorlix, offered to adopt Joseph as a sort of companion. At this age, Joseph would have been less than one foot and nine inches tall (52cm).

In his account of Joseph's life in *Mutants*, Leroi has a rather sunny view of Boruwlaski's subsequent adventures. He suggests that his short stature offered him the chance to escape into a larger and more exciting world.

This may be the right view, but it is not clear that Joseph himself was always entirely happy about the strange course of his life. In his 1820 autobiography, he writes the following melancholy sentence:

'Had it not been for this [being taken up by the Starostin], I should undoubtedly have passed my days in a province on the banks of the Dneistr, where I might have experienced more happiness.'

It is entirely typical of Boruwlaski to think of home and happiness in connection with a river.

Both of Joseph's little siblings were taken up by patronesses. His older brother, who was born around 1728, was four inches (10cm) taller than Joseph, and found a patroness in the Castellane Inowlaska. He was much more than just an amusing companion for her, however. He ended up working as a kind of steward or manager for her whole estate. Joseph's little sister was also adopted by a patroness, and she was even courted by a military officer, but died of small-pox at the age of twenty-two. At her death, she was only two feet and two inches tall (65cm).

It seems that when the Starostin de Caorlix took up Joseph, she was looking for a sort of eternal child to be her companion. Ordinary children grow up and leave home, but what about someone who is obviously not going to grow much at all?

It may have been in the house of the Starostin de Caorlix that Boruwlaski acquired the French nickname 'Joujou'. Denoting, as it does, some kind of doll or toy, the advent of this new name reveals a lot about the Starostin and her attitude to Joseph as a person. The fact that the nickname is French in origin is a reminder of the dominance of French culture and language throughout Europe at the time. In Russia and Poland in particular, the aristocracy used a great deal of French, which was just one of the many things that isolated them from the mass of the people they lorded it over.

Joseph Boruwlaski's time with the Starostin de Caorlix was cut short when that lady, an attractive widow, got married and started to believe that she was pregnant.

Young as he was, Joseph realised that he would probably not be able to compete for the Starostin's affections with a new baby. He started to look for a safe way out of the house of his protectress, who had now acquired the title of Countess de Tarnow through her marriage.

It was at this point that Joseph had a stroke of good luck. Another grand local lady, who bore the traditional Polish title of 'Lady Sword- Bearer', offered him an escape.

At first, Boruwlaski's original protectress didn't want to let him go, but Madame Humieska, whom Boruwlaski always refers to as a countess, deployed an ancient and widely-believed superstition to win Joseph for herself. She reminded her friend that, if a pregnant woman sees a little person, this may cause the baby in her womb to emerge a little person.

Convinced that she might be endangering the future stature of her unborn child, the Countess de Tarnow gave 'Joujou' up to her neighbour the 'Countess' Humieska. This turned out to be not just a stroke of luck, but also a glittering opportunity for Joseph, because his new patroness was determined to travel.

The lure of places such as Vienna must have been very exciting for the Countess and her fifteen-year-old companion, but, in his autobiographies, Joseph implies that part of the attraction of travel for Poles at the time was that it got them out of Poland.

Joseph complains of the inconvenience of travelling on bad Polish roads, with no proper inns along the way. Polish nobles such as Joseph's Countess had to travel with a small army of servants, including scouts to go on in front and look for places to stay for the night. If a likely barn or cabin already had peasants or Jews sleeping in it, these would be unceremoniously turfed out, and a cosy corner made up for the noble traveller, using her own furniture, carpets and hangings.

Poland's problems at this time went far beyond the lack of decent inns. In a travel memoir published in 1800, the English writer Nathaniel Wraxall painted a grim picture of Poland in the latter part of the eighteenth century:

'The Poles, among whom depopulation, oppression, and misery, appear under every possible shape, manifest in their looks and whole appearance the utmost poverty: even the churches are composed of wood, and the hovels of the peasants are of the same materials.'

War contributed its own miseries to the sufferings of ordinary Poles at this time, and indeed Boruwlaski's own brother, a strapping six foot four giant, had been killed in battle along with their uncle. Wraxall was surprised to see such poverty 'in the midst of a soil naturally rich and fertile', and remarked that the Jews seemed to be the only ones who kept industry and commerce alive.

The Countess Humieska's idea of travel was to set aside several years to make a sort of grand progress through the royal courts of Europe. This type of travel was pretty common among the aristocracy of the period.

They would often convey news, presents, greetings, letters, gossip and even state secrets from one great monarch or noble to another, and would find accommodation in the palaces of their contacts, or in grand rented houses.

The Countess's descent from an ancient family practically guaranteed her admittance to the chambers of the great, and she found that curiosity about her tiny companion opened even more doors than might otherwise have been opened for her.

It was a whim of the Countess to dress Joseph like a lieutenant in one of the Polish regiments. It was the fashion for Polish civilian gentlemen at that time to assume military garb, and Joseph continued to wear elaborate red military-style coats for many years.

The first of the gilded capitals Boruwlaski visited on his tour with the Countess was Vienna. This was when Joseph was only fifteen or sixteen years old, and an inch or two over two feet high.

In Vienna, Boruwlaski was presented to the personage he calls the Queen of Hungary, a woman who is better known to history as the Empress Maria Theresa of Austria.

Where other fifteen-year-olds might have been tongue-tied or sullen in the presence of this formidable lady, Joseph immediately won her over with a barrage of flattery. He implied that the Queen's arch-enemy, Frederick the Great of Prussia, should throw himself at her feet. Later, he performed a Polish dance for her and, when she was cuddling him afterwards, he kissed and complimented her hand, and was offered the ring from it.

Unfortunately, the ring was too big for Joseph; but the Queen summoned her little daughter, then five or six years old, whose diamond ring fitted Boruwlaski's finger perfectly. Joseph was delighted with the gift. What the little princess thought is not recorded.

In the 1820 version of his autobiography, Boruwlaski sadly records that the little princess later became known as Marie Antoinette, the Queen of

France who was executed after the French Revolution. This cannot, however, be taken without a pinch of salt.

If we agree with Margot Johnson that Boruwlaski met Maria Theresa in 1752, then Marie Antoinette could not have met Boruwlaski then at all, since she wasn't born until 1755. The date of 1752 doesn't agree with Boruwlaski's account, since that would have made him thirteen at the time, and he says he was fifteen when he was taken up by the Countess Humieska. But even if he had met her in 1755, the future Marie Antoinette would still have been a baby, and certainly not 'about five or six years old'.

Boruwlaski may not have been lying about this. He could easily have got Maria Antonia (as she was called in Austria) mixed up with one of her older sisters. In all, Maria Theresa of Austria had sixteen children, of whom eleven were girls. Amazingly, all the girls had the first name of Maria. Likely candidates for the donation of the ring to Boruwlaski are Maria Johanna (born 1750) and Maria Josepha (1751).

Although it cannot be true that Boruwlaski met Marie Antoinette as a toddler at this time, it does seem to be true that the Empress herself had nice hands.

Despite the jollity he displayed in front of the Empress, Boruwlaski had no illusions about the position he occupied at this time. The truth of this was stripped bare when he overheard a shocking conversation between the Countess Humieska and her friends.

The ladies were debating whether little people could have children, and Boruwlaski's Countess said that she had often wondered what would happen if 'Joujou' were to mate with his own sister, who was also a little person. This dreadful conversation was cut short when Joseph started to cry. But the truth was out: his patroness thought of him as a pet, a toy; hardly a human at all.

After six months in Vienna, Boruwlaski and the Countess proceeded to Munich, then to Lunéville in Lorraine. This was the home of the exiled ex-King of Poland, Stanislaw I. The first Stanislaw was the king to whom Boruwlaski's father had been loyal, which loyalty had lost him his estate on the Dneipr.

That the 'titular King of Poland' should have been living in France, and acting as the master of an estate in the Lorraine, is an indication of the unique character of the Polish political system at the time.

The Poles elected their kings, and in theory any male noble could be elected. Because of the pliable nature of the Polish system, it was easy for foreign powers to interfere with the election of the king; and Stanislaw I himself had been put on the throne by the then King of Sweden, Charles XII.

When Swedish influence began to fade, the previous king, the Saxon Augustus II, regained the throne. When Augustus died in 1733, Stanislaw I tried to return with the support of the French, but his plan was foiled when Russia and Austria invaded. Russia insisted that another Saxon be elected and, in a 1738 treaty, Stanislaw I was given the provinces of Lorraine and Bar in France as a consolation prize.

Boruwlaski claims that Stanislaw I was eighty years old when he met him at Lunéville, which suggests that Boruwlaski and the Countess were there in 1757 (a date which doesn't seem to fit some of the evidence).

Stanislaw's rule in Lorraine struck Boruwlaski as energetic and enlightened, and he particularly liked the architecture of his buildings at Nancy and Lunéville. The court of the exiled King had a reputation for culture, and Stanislaw's writings were considered important enough to be published. He also established military and scientific academies at Lunéville.

Stanislaw I might have been less interested in Boruwlaski than most people, since he already had a little person at his court, called Nicholas Ferry. Despite his English-sounding name, Ferry was actually French.

As it happened, Stanislaw found Boruwlaski fascinating because he was so obviously more intelligent and talented than Ferry, who was nicknamed 'Bébé' and had what we would today call severe learning difficulties.

In keeping a little person at his court, Stanislaw I was following in a tradition that went all the way back to Roman times. The first Roman Emperor, Augustus, is supposed to have had a little person in his household, called Lucius, who was less than two feet (61cm) in height.

Augustus's daughter Julia had a male little person, called Cocopas, and a female one called Andromeda, who was only two feet and four inches tall (70cm). Both Mark Antony and Tiberius had little people in their retinues, and the Emperor Domitian even had a miniature troop of gladiators. The Roman tradition continued until the reign of the Emperor Alexander Severus, who expelled all little people from his court.

Even in societies where slavery was unknown, people of the servant class could in effect be bought and sold, and little people were no exception. At times, the demand for little people outstripped supply, and dealers resorted to cruel ways to restrict the growth of children in order to sell the tragic results. Attempts were also made to breed little people like pigeons or dogs by forcing them to marry other little people.

Court dwarfs were a feature of both the Middle Ages and the Renaissance in Europe. Edgar Allan Poe's short story, *Hop-Frog*, gives a vivid picture of a Medieval hunch-backed court dwarf. The real-life sixteenth-century Italian patroness of the arts, Isabella d'Este of Mantua, had part of her palace made to suit the many little people at her court, and even remembered two of them in her will. The Spanish painter Velasquez produced very penetrating pictures of little people at the court of Philip IV.

The Russian Tsar Peter the Great arranged for two of his little people to marry, and assembled nearly a hundred little wedding guests who rode to the wedding in tiny carriages drawn by Shetland ponies.

Richard Gibson, a little man who was 'page of the back-stairs' at the court of Charles I, was a skilled portrait painter. When he married Anne Shepherd, who was also a little person, the King himself attended the service. The last court dwarf in Britain was Coppernin, who worked for the mother of George III.

The contrast between Stanislaw's 'Bébé' and Joseph Boruwlaski came to the attention of the French Compte de Tressan, a dilettante scientist then staying with the exiled Polish King. The Compte even wrote an encyclopedia article that featured the two little people.

At that time, a group of French scholars was compiling the famous *Encyclopedie*, a serious attempt to gather all human knowledge into one giant, multi-volume reference work. The Encyclopedistes, as the creators of this mighty work were called, welcomed outside contributions from learned men, and the Compte de Tressan contributed their article on Dwarfs (*Nains* in French).

The article is very thin on general scientific information about little people: it is almost entirely taken up with descriptions and potted biographies of Boruwlaski and Nicholas Ferry, and an account of the contrast between them.

The *Encyclopedie* was a child of the eighteenth-century Enlightenment, and, reading between the lines of the article on *Nains*, it is possible to feel the delight of the Compte in having found a man of intelligence and wit among a class of people, the little people, who were once wrongly supposed to be foolish and childish. Even Boruwlaski's comparative lack of education, the Compte implies, can't suppress his rational, enlightened spirit.

The French *Encyclopedie* must rank as one of the great books of the world, alongside Gutenberg's Bible and the First Folio of Shakespeare. For Boruwlaski to have featured in it so prominently is fame indeed.

The *Encyclopedia Britannica*, the later British equivalent of the French *Encyclopedie*, devoted a great deal of space to Boruwlaski in the 'Dwarfs' article of its 1797 edition. The British article draws on the French one of nearly forty years earlier, but it brings Boruwlaski's story up to date. The *Britannica* article includes the enthusiastic sentence:

'Such is this wonderful little man – an object of curiosity really worthy the attention of the philosopher, the man of taste, and the anatomist.'

Nicholas Ferry died in 1764. By this time, when he was only twenty-two years old, his back had grown crooked, and his nose deformed. The King himself cried to hear the news of his little friend's death, but he did agree to the Compte de Tressan's plan to carry out an autopsy. This was conducted by the court physician and his assistants, with the Compte looking on. Nothing unusual was found, except for a large tumour in the brain. Perhaps this was what killed poor Ferry: the tumour may also have had a role in limiting his intelligence.

After the autopsy, Ferry's body were boiled and his skeleton recovered.

In 1980, this was on display at the Musee de l'Homme in Paris. The postmortem treatment of Ferry suggests that if Boruwlaski had died at Lunéville, or at some other court where the scientific craze had taken hold, he too would have been autopsied, boiled and mounted, if his patroness had given permission.

Luckily, when he died in Durham seventy-three years later, Boruwlaski was nobody's servant, and he was given a privileged burial in one of the greatest buildings in the world.

From Lorraine, the Countess Humieska and Boruwlaski proceeded to Versailles, where they delivered letters from Stanislaw I to his daughter, the Queen of France. The Countess and her little friend were received very graciously at Versailles, and managed to become all the rage in Paris.

The Polish Count Michal Oginski, who was then Grand Hetman of Lithuania, was living in Paris at the time and took an interest in Boruwlaski. A noted musician himself, he started to instruct Joseph in music. When he showed promise, Oginski handed him over to Gavinies, a master then living in the French capital, who taught Boruwlaski the guitar.

Short of giving Joseph a pension, Oginski could hardly have done him a bigger favour. Though Joseph didn't need to earn his own money while he was living under the protection of the Countess, his skill on the violin and guitar would be an important source of income to him later, when his patroness disowned him.

Looking back on the beginning of his musical career from the perspective of 1788, Boruwlaski gives us another of his surprising melancholy sentences. He says that his talent on the guitar 'often solaces me in moments of trouble and inquietude, inseparable from a situation like mine'. This paints a picture of Joseph sitting in some lonely corner, with a guitar on his knees, strumming away at a tune to lift his own spirits.

The guitar and violin Boruwlaski owned at his death were both supposed to have been made for him in Vienna, according to the catalogue of his goods that were put up for auction in 1838.

As well as teaching him music, Oginski literally made a centre-piece of Joseph when he gave a grand banquet in Paris. He had Boruwlaski served up in an urn, from which he suddenly sprang, to (nearly) everyone's surprise. Monsieur Bouret, the French Farmer-General, arranged another meal where all the plates, glasses, cutlery and even food was made to be on the same scale as the little Pole. He carefully arranged for small game-birds such as ortolans and becaficos to be served at this dinner.

The Countess found herself rather more in demand in Paris than she might have been, had not Boruwlaski been with her. The Duchess of Modena, who was then in the French capital, was so annoyed at not having seen Boruwlaski that the French Queen had to step in to prevent all-out war between the Duchess and the Countess. From Paris, Boruwlaski and his patroness went on to Holland and Germany, and then to Warsaw, the capital city of their native Poland.

Royal Palace at Warsaw © Miranda Brown

It was at about this time that Joseph Boruwlaski, perhaps ten years later than other boys, began to get interested in girls. And at the age of twenty- five, he began to feel those rebellious and irresponsible feelings that boys experience most powerfully at the age of about fifteen. He became something of a stop-out, mixing with the fast set around the Warsaw theatres.

It is an indication of the character of Polish high culture at this time that the capital was able to support at least one company of French comedians. After some time during which Joseph seems to have fancied every woman he saw, he finally focused his passions on one of the French actresses. His interest in her won him nothing but frustration and public humiliation, but in his 1788 autobiography he looks back on these events with a warm heart.

The Countess sent a very wise older man to talk to Boruwlaski, and as a result Joseph gave up the company of the disreputable young men with whom he had been associating. It may have been at this time that he also gave up drinking anything but water.

But he could not give up his interest in women, even though he was quite aware that his unusual appearance might be a hindrance to him in that area.

In the 1788 version of his autobiography, Boruwlaski writes about his feelings at this time with startling frankness. Most adolescent boys must have doubts about whether they will ever be able to appeal to any woman, but Joseph's size made this feeling of unworthiness, and of inability to compete with his peers, particularly intense.

In his 1820 autobiography he is much less explicit

about his romantic urges, perhaps because European culture had become more buttoned-up by that time.

No longer able to pursue French actresses away from home, Joseph found a sort of Frenchwoman to act as an object for his affections, in the Countess's house in Warsaw. This was Isalina Barboutan, the darkly beautiful daughter of a middle-class French couple who lived in the Polish capital. The Countess had taken her on as a companion and lady-in-waiting, and Boruwlaski fell in love with her.

At first, Isalina laughed at his professions of love, but he showered her with passionate love-letters, and at last she agreed to marry him.

The remaining obstacle was the Countess. She was furious, and it is tempting to speculate on exactly why the courtship of her two protégés should have made her so angry. Perhaps, like Boruwlaski's first protectress, the Starostina de Caorlix, Countess Humieska thought of Joseph as a sort of substitute child. His wishing to get married was a sign of maturity that spoiled her picture of him. Or perhaps she wanted to arrange a more glittering marriage for Isalina.

Joseph's marital ambitions caused the Countess to disown him. Having lived in luxury and moved among the most wealthy and famous people of Europe, he now found himself with no income and a wife-to-be to support, since Isalina was also cast out.

Isalina's decision to, in effect, elope with Joseph must have come out of pure love for the little man. As a lady-in-waiting to an aristocratic patroness, Isalina could have expected to catch the eye of some well-off, eligible nobleman from the Countess's social circle. She might even have ended up as mistress of large estates, in Poland or elsewhere in Europe.

This would have been even more likely in her case as everyone agreed that she was very beautiful.

Isalina could have had no illusions about Boruwlaski's prospects, since she occupied a similar position to his in the Countess's household. It might be argued that she was attracted by his rank as a nobleman, but the cheeky way she spoke to him when he first declared his love does not suggest that she looked up to him socially.

Luckily, the newly-elected King of Poland took an interest in the fate of Isalina and Joseph. He approved of their planned nuptials and granted Boruwlaski an annuity of one hundred ducats. Soon the pair were married, and launched on a completely new sort of life.

4. The Wandering Minstrel

A wandering minstrel I -
A thing of shreds and patches,
Of ballads, songs and snatches,
And dreamy lullaby!

W.S. Gilbert, The Mikado

It soon became clear that Joseph and his new wife could not live on the small annuity that the King of Poland had granted to Boruwlaski. After six weeks, Isalina was pregnant, and the situation seemed desperate. The King's brother Kazimierz suggested that Boruwlaski should travel to other courts and cities, to look for opportunities of further sources of income.

With this end in mind, the King provided the newlyweds with a coach.

It may seem strange that the King of Poland should have taken such an interest in the couple, who were of comparatively low social status. That he should have been generous enough to give Boruwlaski an annuity, as well as one of his coaches, is surely an act of real disinterested generosity.

This sort of thing was, however, entirely typical of King Stanislaw II of Poland, who was a terrible spendthrift, and a man who never really understood the value of money. He may also have sympathised with Boruwlaski's plight, because he himself had been disappointed in love. As a young man, he had had a passionate and dangerous affair with the future Russian Empress, Catherine the Great. The pair even had a child, which unfortunately died in infancy.

Politics forced Stanislaw and Catherine apart, and though he hoped for many years that he might eventually be able to marry her, she went on to treat both Stanislaw and his country most cruelly. She never seems to have entertained the marriage idea for long, even after her husband Tsar Peter III died in mysterious circumstances in 1762.

Stanislaw was a very approachable king, a trait that he modelled on what he knew of the sixteenth century French king, Henri IV. But Henri had saved his country from disintegration by putting an end to a ruinous war, whereas Stanislaw II presided over a Poland that was first cut to pieces, then lost as an independent country for over a century.

Stanislaw II particularly liked to meet foreigners, and Poles who had travelled in foreign lands, as he had done. Boruwlaski and Isalina might have appealed to him because, although she had been born in Poland, she still counted as a sort of Frenchwoman; and Boruwlaski had already travelled widely by that time.

Stanislaw was also very partial to beautiful women, and the sight of Isalina in distress could easily have melted his heart.

The Boruwlaskis now travelled to Kracow, the old capital of Poland, where Isalina gave birth to a girl. Boruwlaski saw that this beautiful city had become, in effect, a frontier town on the border between the remaining part of Poland, and the huge tranche of the country that had been taken over by the Austrians. Similar areas had been occupied by Russia and Prussia, in what was called the First Partition of Poland, in 1772. The part seized by the Austrians included Joseph's home province of Galicia.

This was the beginning of the end for the Polish state, the remaining part of which was so heavily influenced by Russia that it couldn't really be regarded as independent. It was Russia that had put Stanislaw II on the throne. Though he worked hard for reform under the shadow of the Russian eagle, Stanislaw was a puppet king, and everybody in Europe expected his country to be completely swallowed up at last by the powerful states that surrounded it.

From Kracow, Boruwlaski, Isalina and the new baby set out for Vienna, with the coach now mounted on a sledge, and arrived on the eleventh of February, 1781. Joseph was now forty-two years old: his wife is thought to have been about fifteen years younger.

The Empress Maria Theresa, whose hands Boruwlaski had complimented nearly thirty years before, had just died, and the Austrian capital was in deep mourning. There was, however, a court of sorts held in the *hotel* of the Prince de Kaunitz.

Boruwlaski was soon mixing in the highest circles again, but nobody was offering him a pension or ready money. It was then that he decided he should give a concert, and make money, for the first time, by his own labour.

His court connections managed to clear the schedule of a local theatre for him, and Boruwlaski gave a well-attended show. The advice of the French and the British ambassadors at Vienna convinced him that, despite his aristocratic misgivings about becoming a man for hire, he should continue to give concerts, and should, in effect, go on tour. The British Ambassador, Sir Gilbert Murray Keith, convinced him that he should go to Britain, where he said he was sure to make a fortune.

His pockets full of letters of recommendation, Boruwlaski set off for Presburg, the capital of Hungary, then doubled back to the Austrian town of Linz. Here the Count de Thierheim, 'Governor of Low Austria', lent the wandering Pole his own band of musicians to pad out the concert, which was not a financial success. It was at this concert that the Countess de Thierheim, then only six or seven years old, begged her father to buy Joseph for her, as if he were a little doll or pet.

Not being for sale in quite that way, Boruwlaski continued on to the German city of Ratisbon, where he was unable to give a concert, then to Munich, where he was a great success. Here His Serene Highness the Elector arranged the concert, covered the costs himself, and moreover gave Joseph an extra gift of money. The Empress Dowager also gave him a gold box filled with ducats.

For more than twenty years, Joseph Boruwlaski wandered in this way around the towns and cities of Continental Europe and the British Isles, hob-nobbing with the rich and famous, being seen at dinners and dances, and trying to get his aristocratic acquaintances to help him arrange concerts. He always seems to have tried to leave each place with letters of recommendation, and other communications, which had to be delivered personally to the next emperor, empress, king, queen, duke, duchess or margrave he planned to visit.

Whether Boruwlaski was any good as a musician is an interesting question. According to his autobiographies, many people praised his music, and we have the independent testimonies of his friends William Burdon and Catherine Hutton, who both thought him excellent.

Boruwlaski's own accounts of his concerts usually concentrate on their success or otherwise as social occasions and as money-making opportunities, not as musical performances.

In his autobiographies, Boruwlaski never mentions a single specific piece of music that he performed, and he also refrains from even telling us which instrument he played where, or whether he played guitar for part of a concert, and violin for the rest.

Although he wrote and published a piano piece, *The Volunteer*, in his later years at Durham, we don't know if any of the pieces he played in his concerts were his own original compositions, the works of other composers, popular 'folk' tunes, or improvised pieces. Since he learned guitar at first from Count Michal Oginski, it may be that his repertoire included some pieces written by that count, who was a noted composer.

Boruwlaski was said to be a good dancer of traditional Polish dances, so perhaps he included dance tunes, or even his own dancing, in his concerts.

The financial success or otherwise of Boruwlaski's concerts depended on a lot of factors, most of which had nothing to do with music. If he couldn't ingratiate himself with some powerful local person, he might not be able to stage a concert at all. If his powerful friend paid all his expenses and expected no share of the profits, he might make a fortune – but if he had to lay out large sums just to secure a venue, then he might leave a town or city seriously out of pocket.

Even if Boruwlaski was an excellent musician, it is likely that some of the people who attended his concerts did not do so for strictly musical reasons. Sometimes the presence of the local big-wig was guaranteed, in which case the concert would become an unmissable date in the social calendar. And some people with no interest in music probably bought tickets just so that they could see the 'celebrated Polish dwarf'.

On the road, the Boruwlaski family ran the risk of highwaymen, bad roads and weather, and the machinations of unscrupulous inn-keepers and theatre-owners. The political and military upheavals at the time presented their own risks. On one occasion, Boruwlaski walked right into a revolution: later, he found himself in the middle of a military invasion.

Although Boruwlaski had previously met some of the people who helped him give concerts, he often found himself relying on the kindness of strangers. The Margrave of Anspach, at Trierdorff, was particularly kind, and offered to take care of the

Boruwlaskis' daughter while they were travelling. After passing through Frankfurt, Mainz, Mannheim, Strasburg and Brussels, Boruwlaski and his wife set off from Ostend for England.

After a stormy passage during which the weather delayed them for four sea-sick days, the couple reached Margate on the twentieth of March 1782.

Boruwlaski was armed with a priceless letter of recommendation addressed to the Duke and Duchess of Devonshire. This particular duchess, the celebrated Georgiana, has recently become better-known through a popular biography by Amanda Foreman and a film starring Keira Knightley. Georgiana was a famous (though unconventional) beauty, a leader of fashion, a dabbler in politics, a drinker and a terrible gambler.

The Devonshires became, in effect, Boruwlaski's new patrons, at least for the first few months of their stay in England. The Duchess rented rooms for them and paid for a doctor to visit the ailing Isalina. This physician, a Dr Walker, somehow failed to recognise that Boruwlaski was a little person at first, and took him for a child. In his relation of this incident, Boruwlaski reveals that the doctor was further confused by Boruwlaski's voice, which seemed to be too deep for someone of his stature.

The Duke of Devonshire sent Boruwlaski a suit specially made to his proportions. This included a coat embroidered with silver and gems, and a steel sword. Through the Devonshires, Boruwlaski was introduced for the first time to the Prince of Wales, who later become Prince Regent, and then King George IV. The Prince was a close friend of Georgiana, and some suspect that they may have been lovers. After their meeting, the Prince sent Boruwlaski a 'pretty little watch'. He showed a lack of imagination (or memory) when he met Joseph many years later, and presented him with another watch.

Boruwlaski's conquest of English high society was so rapid that less than a month after his queasy arrival at Margate, he was spending four hours with the King and Queen and a selection of their children. He was struck by a dangerous fever almost immediately afterwards – one of the few instances of personal illness that he ever alludes to in his autobiographies – and the King's physician was sent to treat him.

Despite his social success, Boruwlaski was soon out of pocket again, and forced to resume his practice of trying to earn money through concerts. The most promising places for him to try were the various assembly rooms: these were a feature of British life that once seemed indispensable, but which has now nearly disappeared.

Joseph Boruwlaski's first London concert was at Carlisle House in Soho, where he had to lay out no less than eighty guineas in advance (worth over £5000 today). The concert was, nevertheless, a financial success, but the failure of a subsequent concert there showed that Boruwlaski hadn't yet caught on to the pattern of the London social season. He nearly made a loss from the second concert, because his aristocratic audience had nearly all repaired to their homes in the country.

Carlisle House was a set of assembly rooms which had acquired a slightly tawdry, raffish reputation during the eventful reign of its first manager, the enterprising Theresa Cornelys. The establishment had once offered balls, teas, suppers, concerts and even operas, all in rooms decorated in the latest fashion. By the time Joseph appeared there, it was in its last days: Mrs Cornelys had bankrupted herself and been forced to hand over her creation to her creditors.

The following winter, Boruwlaski proved to be quite a hit at the spa town of Bath, but on returning to London he found to his horror that his patroness, the Duchess of Devonshire, would not see him. He was so dismayed that he even became ill again, and was immensely relieved when Georgiana gave birth to a child. It seems that even this broad-minded Duchess believed the old superstition that if one saw a little person when pregnant, one's own child might turn out to be a little person. This was why she wouldn't see him when she was expecting.

It was foolish of Georgiana to entertain this pseudo-medical superstition, but one can hardly blame her for being nervous about the health of her unborn child. She had had many miscarriages in the first years of her marriage, and the baby born in 1783, Lady Georgiana Cavendish, was the first child she carried to term.

By this time, Boruwlaski was exhibiting himself for a five-shilling admittance charge (about £15 today). This was something Boruwlaski hated doing, resorted to only reluctantly and didn't like to write about. At times, he tried to disguise these 'visits' as ordinary social soirées, and his gawking guests were assured that the five shillings was just a generous tip for his valet. He sometimes used Gould's Hotel in London's Jermyn Street as a venue for the visits, but

Hargreaves, in his book on the Little Count, suggests that he continued the practice at his home in Durham.

To judge from the engraving which acts as a frontispiece to Boruwlaski's 1788 autobiography, he had furniture made to his own scale, so these pieces might have added to the appeal of the exhibition. He must have been aware, however, that these 'visits' put him dangerously close to the level of the bearded ladies, Irish giants, contortionists and people with disabilities who had been displayed in fairground tents throughout Europe for centuries. Eighteenth-century London offered such fascinating attractions as conjoined twins, a 'North American savage', a satyr, and even a mermaid, who was exhibited for money at Charing Cross.

Although five shillings was a lot of money at the end of the eighteenth century, Boruwlaski's income was still not sufficient. He needed to try music again. He gave another concert, this time at Gallini's Assembly Rooms, a rival venue to Carlisle House. This was an altogether classier place to perform: run by a well-connected ex-dancer, Gallini's in Hanover Square was an extremely prestigious musical venue at the time. King George III attended Gallini's concerts so often that he even had an extra little room installed there, where he could take tea with his wife Queen Charlotte. Unfortunately, the King's mental health problems exhibited themselves during some concerts, when he was seen to be copying out the programme again and again in his own handwriting. Other famous names associated with Gallini's in its heyday included John Christian Bach (son of J.S. Bach).

Boruwlaski's status as a foreigner with a very un-English surname would have done him nothing but good in terms of bums on seats at his concerts in London. Much of the musical culture of the Metropolis at this time was in the hands of foreign immigrants. Gallini himself was Italian Swiss, and Theresa Cornelys was Viennese. The musical stars Cornelys had once employed included not only J.C. Bach, but also Karl Abel, Stephano Storace, Karl Weichsell and Guardagni, none of whom sound particularly British. Then as now, all aspects of British culture benefited from the influence of talented foreigners.

With the profits from his concert at Gallini's, Boruwlaski paid for a passage to Ireland, in April 1783. But before he even reached Ireland, he was seriously inconvenienced by the actions of a supposed Marquis. This impostor was quite happy to take money from, and waste the time of, such a defenceless creature as Joseph. The unnamed 'parasite' (as Joseph called him) promised to prepare the ground for Boruwlaski in Ireland, where, he assured him, he would be such a great success that he would be able to retire on an annuity.

The 'Marquis' crossed the Irish Sea first. Boruwlaski arrived in Dublin two weeks later and was bitterly disappointed to find him living in an inn near the port, presumably spending the poor Pole's money on an idle life. Eventually, Boruwlaski had to pay him to go back to England.

While Joseph tried to rescue his Irish adventure from its unpromising start, Isalina was forced to stay in London because of a sickness which, it seems, had not completely vanished when she crossed to Ireland four months later. Meanwhile Boruwlaski got back into his stride and took Dublin by storm, receiving subsidies from the titled people, and giving a brilliant concert at the Rotunda.

© The Rotunda Hospital, Dublin

Like Carlisle House and Gallini's in London, the Rotunda was a top-drawer set of assembly rooms where concerts could be given. The attached gardens and the assembly rooms themselves, with their distinctive round concert-hall, had been built as a source of income for the adjacent lying-in hospital. With its magnificent Corinthian pilasters and distinguished Dublin clientèle, the Rotunda was surely Joseph's sort of place.

By the time Boruwlaski left Dublin for Newry and Drogheda, his wife was back with him, but now she was both ill and pregnant. When they returned to

Dublin, sea-bathing was recommended as a cure, but while Isalina and her daughter were on the coast, it seems that a servant called Francis Lombardi robbed them of goods worth over sixty guineas (nearly £4000 today).

If the Boruwlaskis were really carrying such valuable stuff around with them, it is hardly surprising. They had no permanent home, and in those days proper banking services were reserved for the rich. Joseph himself was also regularly given expensive gifts, which he may not have wanted to exchange for currency straight away, since they were, many of them, glittering tokens of regard from his distinguished patrons.

He might have hesitated to convert these goods into bank-notes, since the same currency was not accepted everywhere. Even within England, Bank of England notes were sometimes viewed with suspicion in parts of the provinces, where local banks printed their own money.

Having re-crossed the Irish Sea, Boruwlaski remained in Liverpool for a time, vainly hoping that his treasures would be returned to him from Ireland.

At Oxford, a mysterious gentleman invited Boruwlaski to come and dine at a house a few miles away. The house was Blenheim Palace, and his hosts the Duke and Duchess of Marlborough. The Duke begged Joseph for one of his tiny shoes, which he placed in his collection.

The Duke of Marlborough was not alone in his enthusiasm for collecting strange things. Many titled and learned people at this time had collections of interesting objects: these collections were sometimes called cabinets of curiosities.

We know that shoes of Boruwlaski's got into the collections of the Duke of Marlborough and of King George IV. The odd thing is that both Marlborough and King George asked for only one shoe. What did they expect Joseph to do with the other one?

Boruwlaski returned to London in 1786, after an absence of three years.

There he met up with his old friend, teacher and patron Count Oginski, who in effect made a generous donation by paying for a concert and allowing Boruwlaski to take all the profits.

It was in London in 1788 that Boruwlaski tried a new way to make money: publishing his autobiography by subscription.

According to Samuel Johnson, in his *Lives of the Poets*, the publishing of books by subscription was an idea first tried by the English poet John Dryden.

Dryden contemplated making an English verse translation of the *Aeneid*, an epic poem by the Roman poet Virgil. He persuaded subscribers to give him money 'up front' and arranged with the printer to sell copies only to the subscribers. As an added bonus, the subscribers had their names printed in the front of the book: this gave them a little taste of immortality, and the status of patrons of literature.

This seems to have been the procedure followed by Joseph Boruwlaski, and the result was a handsome volume incorporating his own words in French on the left-hand page of each opening, and an English translation on the right.

Frontispiece to the 1788 Memoirs (DCC)

The frontispiece is a stipple-engraving by W. Hinks of Boruwlaski with his wife and one of their daughters. Although only what we would now call a toddler, the child seems to be larger than her father, but the artist has made an error in perspective: it is hard to see exactly how big Joseph is supposed to be, or where he is standing in relation to his little family.

The proud father is wearing an eighteenth-century wig similar in style to the ones still worn by lawyers in British law-courts even today. He also wears a sword, in keeping with the military style of his costume. Isalina is very fashionably dressed, in a huge hat with outsized feathers, perched on an improbably puffed-up coiffure. Her hair must be heavily powdered, since her eyebrows are still dark.

The family is pictured against a conventional background of heavy, dark curtains which suggest a grimly luxurious domestic setting. Light streams down from an unseen source at top right – standing where he appears to be, Joseph should probably be literally in the shadow of his wife, but somehow the shadow manages to stop at his feet.

The picture is not a work of genius, and the figure of Joseph himself is so poorly proportioned that it strays close to crude caricature. In particular, his eyes, his left hand and his right foot are too large, and the arrangement of the legs is just a bad error of drawing. The stipple effect which is characteristic of this type of engraving gives a swirling and indistinct feel to large areas of the picture. The artist has given Boruwlaski an expression of manic simpering, while Isalina looks tired, bored, timid and vain all at the same time. Given her later treatment of Boruwlaski, this might actually be an accurate representation of her feelings.

Publishing his autobiography by subscription did not bring Boruwlaski the fortune he perhaps expected. There were various things that could go wrong with this method of raising money, including the unauthorised printing of extra copies by unscrupulous printers. This was a problem in the case of Dryden's *Aeneid*, and the fact that potential subscribers knew they might not have exclusive access to the new book may have made them less keen to pay a lot of money up-front.

Hiring an engraver and a translator might also have made a hole in the profits, and Boruwlaski may also have spent all his share of the subscribers' money long before he had finished writing. This seems likely, since towards the end of the book, Joseph frankly declares that he is broke, and needs help. He may even have sold his share in the profits expected after publication, in return for some money to tide him over. His financial situation seems to have been particularly bad at this time, since groundless rumours of his great wealth had reached Poland, and Stanislaw II had stopped his annuity.

The book is an important source for students of Boruwlaski's life, but Boruwlaski did not use the writing of it just to lay bare the truth of his years. He also used the book as an opportunity to describe the kindness of his various benefactors, and to thank them once again. These sometimes very fulsome thanks are closely linked to Boruwlaski's shameless name-dropping habit, and give the book a very polite, old-fashioned atmosphere.

The problem with the name-dropping is that, in

many cases, the names he drops would have impressed his first readers, but are by no means widely known today.

Boruwlaski was forced to continue his life as a wandering minstrel. At Norwich, he tried to get the celebrated actress Mrs Siddons to appear with him, but she declined to do so. This brush-off did not prevent Boruwlaski being great friends with her brother, the actor Stephen Kemble, in later life.

It was in Norwich that Boruwlaski met the famous comedian Charles Mathews. Mathews generously agreed to cancel a performance of his own in the town, so that audiences would not be drawn away from Boruwlaski's concert. Boruwlaski and Mathews became firm friends, and Mathews' second wife Frances included valuable material about Boruwlaski in her memoir of the comedian.

Also in Norwich, the mysterious Mrs B__ tried to start a subscription for Boruwlaski, which would have enabled him to live comfortably without the need of endless travelling and concerts. The subscription idea fell through – Boruwlaski tells us this was due to the machinations of a cunning Frenchman called 'Dertreval'. The real name of this person was perhaps de Trouville. This was also the surname of one of Isalina's uncles: were these people one and the same?

Thanks to a letter of introduction from his friend Miss Metcalfe, Boruwlaski proved a great hit when he arrived in Cambridge, where he gave what he calls a 'brilliant' concert. After Cambridge, he went to visit the country seat of Miss Metcalfe near Bury St Edmund's, in which town he also gave a concert. Carrying another letter of recommendation,

Boruwlaski was then to score another hit at Edinburgh.

Travelling south again with a plan to return to France, Boruwlaski gave successful concerts at York and Bath. In Boulogne, Boruwlaski managed to make his concert pay, but at Lisle the owner of the theatre kept the profits for himself. In Paris, Boruwlaski found himself witnessing the beginning of the French Revolution, and was unable to make money by any means. He returned to England via Guernsey, where, with the help of those magic letters of recommendation, he was able to continue giving concerts.

At Coventry, the Mayor asked for five pounds in return for permission to give a concert, and Boruwlaski, being very light in pocket at the time, was obliged to creep out of the town at five o'clock the next morning.

Five pounds then would be worth nearly £170 today.

At Birmingham, a Methodist landlord called Mr Sharp insisted that Boruwlaski pay a bill that was many pounds above what seemed reasonable. Clearly, as in the case of the theatre-owner of Lisle, Sharp was taking advantage of the fact that a tiny person like Boruwlaski could not offer any physical resistance – Sharp could probably have kicked him across the room without much effort.

It was also in Birmingham that Boruwlaski made another friend who was to last him many years – in this case a young lady called Catherine Hutton. She wrote an account of Joseph's life in an article for *Bentley's Miscellany*. *Bentley's* was a popular periodical, founded in 1837, the year of Joseph's death. No less a writer than Charles Dickens was its first editor, and it survives today in the form of bound volumes. Catherine Hutton's article is included in the 1845 volume of *Bentley's*, and it opens with a clear statement about Joseph's status as a count:

'Joseph Boruwlaski was not a count; nor did he ever personally assume this title; his father was a gentleman, but a poor one.'

Since Hutton's article was published eight years after Boruwlaski's death, we can hardly accuse her of exploding Joseph's 'count' myth with any malicious intent. If, as Hannah Swiderska asserts, Boruwlaski started to call himself a count whilst in Birmingham, then his Birmingham friend Catherine Hutton may have been privy to the miraculous process of Joseph's blood becoming just a little bluer. Swiderska's 1968 article for the Polish newspaper *Wiadomósci* can be read in English translation at the Palace Green University library in Durham.

Much of Catherine Hutton's article on Boruwlaski is based on one or more of Boruwlaski's autobiographies, but she is also able to give first-hand details about his first stay in Birmingham, which began towards the end of 1785. It seems that Boruwlaski, his wife and Isalina's uncle rented a house belonging to Hutton's father during their stay in Birmingham. The uncle's name was Monsieur de Trouville, which suggests that he may have been the same person who did Boruwlaski out of some money around this time.

Boruwlaski was exhibiting himself for money again, but, unlike the Londoners, the people of Birmingham only had to pay one shilling, and not five. The Huttons paid their shilling, and subsequently invited Joseph for Christmas dinner, then to tea and supper every week. It was after one of these suppers that the newly-minted Count played the guitar and danced at the same time. For any other man nearing fifty, this would have been quite a feat. At the Huttons', Isalina also sang French songs.

Boruwlaski clearly felt at home with this Birmingham family, because when they didn't have other guests for him to entertain, he could relax, show his true self and sit sad and silent by the fire.

Catherine admired Isalina and admitted that she was beautiful and 'quite a Frenchwoman', but could not find it in her heart to like her:

'She was a woman whom any man might love, but certainly not a woman whom it was prudent for Boruwlaski to marry.'

This is a rather mysterious thing to say, and it gives rise to speculations about Mrs Boruwlaski's character. At worst, it suggests that Isalina was having affairs with other men. At best, it may be that Catherine Hutton found that her manners were just not as polished as Joseph's, which she found uniquely admirable.

It was after Boruwlaski left Birmingham for the first time that Isalina disappeared from his life. Since one of her uncles was with them around this time, it may be that she took the opportunity to go with him back to France, or perhaps to Poland. Margot Johnson tells us that Boruwlaski returned to Poland for a brief visit during these years, and it may be that Isalina went with him, and then decided to stay put. If we prefer a more sensational story, we can imagine that she was swept off her feet by some handsome officer.

In any case, we mustn't be too hard on Isalina for deserting her husband. It is clear from her many illnesses that constant travel didn't agree with her, and we know that poverty and an uncertain income doesn't agree with anyone. She might have felt more involved in her husband's life if she herself had taken the role of manager or agent, but she never seems to have asserted herself in that way, despite the fact that she had acquired better English than Boruwlaski.

It would have taken a bold woman, in those days, to have taken an active role in the acquisition of her husband's income, but there certainly were women who did such things. In any event, Isalina Boruwlaski seems to have died at around this time, since we have a record of her husband telling George IV, in 1821, that she had been dead for thirty years.

According to an 1807 book called *The Eccentric Mirror*, written by G.H. Wilson, Joseph told one Daniel Lambert that he didn't really grieve for his wife, as she had had the habit of putting him on top of a cupboard when she was annoyed with him.

The meeting between Boruwlaski and Lambert, which happened in 1802, must have been something to see. Lambert was a famously overweight man, who would have weighed about forty-nine stones in

1802 (over 311 kilos or 686 pounds). Like Boruwlaski, Lambert was also forced to make money by exhibiting himself for a shilling.

In 1792 Boruwlaski turned once again to the plan of publishing his autobiography by subscription. The second edition, published in Birmingham, is nicely printed, but the copy I have seen is on poor-quality woodchip paper – the type where bits of wood are still visible in the texture of the paper itself. This copy, which belongs to Durham University, is especially precious, though, because it has Boruwlaski's own handwriting in the front. The copy was inscribed by Boruwlaski himself to a Mr Hoy – probably the same Hoy who is listed among the subscribers to the 1820 autobiography. The inscription is in French, which suggests that Hoy could read French, otherwise the 1792 autobiography would have been of no use to him: this version was printed entirely in the French language, with no translation.

It may be that Boruwlaski had mislaid the English version of his book, or feared that, if he printed it, he would have to pay something to the translator. It may be that he wished to include new material in the 1792 autobiography, and did not want to engage anyone to produce a new translation.

Whether a book written entirely in French would have attracted many buyers in Birmingham at the end of the eighteenth century is hard to say.

The dedication to Hoy in the Durham University copy suggests that Boruwlaski certainly hadn't sold out.

A new frontispiece engraving shows Boruwlaski *solus*, once again wearing his military-style coat, with a miniature sabre strapped to his side.

Although he was by this time fifty-three years old, the picture makes Joseph look younger and slimmer than he did in the frontispiece of the 1788 autobiography. It shows him standing by a small, round table, with his guitar resting on the table itself.

In the absence of any other people in the picture, the engraver has relied on the table alone to give a sense of scale, and an idea of Joseph's smallness. For the first time, we see the slightly top-heavy character of Boruwlaski's shape, an effect caused by his large head and small feet.

The Reinagle portrait
© The Hunterian Museum, Royal College of Surgeons

This top-heaviness is a feature of the full-length portrait made by Phillip Reinagle for the surgeon John Hunter's medical museum. According to information from the Royal College of Surgeons, which now owns the picture, this painting could not have been painted after 1793, and to judge from the apparent age of Joseph in the picture, it was probably painted at around the same time as the 1792 frontispiece.

Like the 1792 engraving, Reinagle's picture shows Joseph in his military jacket, complete with sword and powdered wig – or at least powdered hair. Whereas the engraving uses a table to give scale, Reinagle employs a chair, against one arm of which Boruwlaski leans. His expression in this picture is defiant, even pugnacious. Perhaps his desertion by his wife, or his constant money troubles, gave him this clouded expression, or perhaps he knew that this painting was intended for a museum of medical curiosities, and would be gawped at by medical students.

Joseph must have been something of a challenge to the numerous eighteenth-century artists who made pictures of him. In those days, it was usual for artists to employ lay-figures – carefully proportioned poseable dolls -to stand in for the subject of a portrait. Such lay-figures could not have been used in Joseph's case, so the portraitists must have been forced to paint Joseph properly – from life.

Joseph journeyed to Ireland again, some time in the 1790s, and this time he was not duped by any unscrupulous parasites. The captain of the ship in which he crossed the Irish Sea took care to help

Boruwlaski settle his accommodation arrangements in advance, so that he could not become the victim of another landlord like the aptly-named Sharp.

At Cork, Boruwlaski became the talk of the town because of a comical misunderstanding caused by his imperfect English. From something a Mrs McLennel said to him, he understood that the brother of the French revolutionary Mirabeau would be paying him a visit at his lodgings. But Mrs McLennel was a butcher's wife, and sent him, not a French aristocrat, but some *marrow-bone* soup. After that, everyone in the town sent him marrow-bone soup, and, ever conscious of his health, Joseph began to fear that he would become 'as fat as marrow'.

While visiting the lake of Killarney, Boruwlaski gave another demonstration of his talent for outrageous flirtation and flattery. As he clambered around the rocks near the Devil's Punch-Bowl, a lady cried out, 'Take care, that that little gentleman does not fall!'

'Madam, I fall already,' said the Count, seeing that the lady was a 'lovely nymph'. With the help of the nymph, who was called Mrs Brown, and her husband, the town of Limerick was charmed into giving Boruwlaski another successful concert.

At Clonmel in Tipperary Boruwlaski found a type of people with whom one would not flirt, and who, in those days, would not have welcomed a concert. This was a community of Quakers, who gave the Count a very warm welcome. They impressed Joseph with their quiet and humane way of life.

The Quakers of Clonmel were central to the textile industry there, and in those days they would have looked and acted very differently from many of the people Boruwlaski usually mixed with. They would have worn Plain Dress – modest, drab-coloured garments without unnecessary embellishment. They would also have used Plain Speech, addressing Boruwlaski as 'thee' or 'thou' rather than 'you', which was supposed to be more respectful. Among them, the teetotal Joseph would not have had to turn down offers of alcoholic drink, since they probably didn't drink either.

On a Sunday in Ballinasloe, Boruwlaski came across an altogether noisier type of Christianity, when he walked up to a group of Methodists who were hymn-singing in the street. The hymn broke off while they all gawped at him, and their frustrated preacher cried out, 'Brethren, my dear brethren, return to your duty, and don't follow this red devil'. Boruwlaski happened to be wearing his usual red military jacket at the time.

On the road to Galway, on a dark, snowy night, Boruwlaski was obliged to seek shelter in the home of a poor but hospitable Irishman, whose cabin was already full of people sleeping on straw. This must have reminded Joseph of the rough conditions travellers sometimes encountered in his native Poland, but before he could doze off, he was invited to the house of an anonymous gentleman.

This fine house, with its excellent dinner, musical diversions and feather-beds, made Boruwlaski think he was in Paradise. Next morning, he took the opportunity to look around the place. As usual, the water- features in the gardens particularly caught his attention. Reflected in the lake, the house, he thought, looked like a temple of Apollo. Was it this mysterious Irish house that stuck in his mind and gave him the idea for his own riverside temple decades later?

Another attempt was made to do the Count out of some money at Galway, but this time Boruwlaski had with him an Irish servant, called Noad. This brave fellow was prepared to knock down the crafty landlord, one McDule, if he persisted in his dishonesty. Boruwlaski decided it would be better to employ a cunning plan to escape McDule's clutches.

One night, acting on Boruwlaski's instructions, Noad deliberately got into a fight with McDule, then simulated an injury using fake blood.

Noad's cry of 'Murder!' woke the whole house, and McDule waived Boruwlaski's rent in order to avoid being arrested for assault. In other words, while Boruwlaski arranged concerts throughout Ireland, in Galway he stage-managed a farce.

Whereas in Ballinasloe, Boruwlaski's appearance had disrupted the singing of a Methodist hymn, at Sligo he practically started a riot. He came into the town on the morning of a great pig-fair, and before he even got into the centre, a large number of curious people was following him.

A huge crowd gathered round him when he stopped in the midst of the fair, and he feared he would never escape, but luckily a number of pigs escaped, and he was able to slip away in the confusion.

Boruwlaski was probably in Ireland when his home country of Poland ceased to exist as an independent state. In the Second Partition of 1793, Russia and Prussia took further immense swathes of land. In the Third Partition of 1795, the remainder was swallowed up and Boruwlaski's patron, King Stanislaw II, became a virtual prisoner in the Russian capital, St Petersburg.

The hopes of the Polish nation had not, however, died for all time. When a great military leader called Napoleon Bonaparte started to rearrange the map of Europe, many Poles flocked to his standard and joined the so-called Polish Legions. They hoped that by fighting for the Corsican, they would oblige him to help them win back their country.

Meanwhile, in various towns and cities in Ireland, Boruwlaski was able to stage successful concerts, but his expectations of a hit at Athlone were frustrated by the French General Lazare Hoche, who chose the night of his concert to invade the country.

The threat of invasion caused all the people of Athlone to lock themselves in their houses, and Boruwlaski found himself thrown into the company of his landlord, an apothecary. As Boruwlaski had an abiding interest in chemistry, his conversations with the apothecary of Athlone might have entertained him, except that the man's only real interest was in his own formula for pickling beef. As soon as he could, Boruwlaski escaped to the nearby city of Longford.

Hoche's 1796 invasion attempt was a French response to requests for help from rebellious Catholic Irishmen, including the famous Wolfe Tone.

In the end, the invasion was a complete failure: the French Armada was scattered by storms, and no troops were landed. Many of the Irish rebels were hauled off to Australia, and the British used the excuse to bring in the Act of Union, whereby

Ireland could be ruled directly from Westminster.

Like Poland, Ireland had become even more of a subject nation.

Boruwlaski returned to England via the Isle of Man, crossed Cumberland, found nothing to interest him in Carlisle, and fetched up in Newcastle, where he gave a very successful concert, together with some amateur musicians. In Newcastle, Captain Archibald Dickson, R.N., advised him to go to Durham (it was at Dickson's house that Joseph met Daniel Lambert in 1802). Dickson gave Boruwlaski a letter of introduction to Thomas Ebdon of Durham. This was probably the most useful letter of introduction that Joseph ever got.

Ebdon was a Durham man, born and bred; the son of a shoemaker, baptised at St Oswald's on Church Street and married at St Nicholas's in the Market Place. He served as organist at the Cathedral for nearly sixty years, and made extra money by organising concerts in Durham.

At one time, Ebdon had actually lived in the Assembly Rooms in Durham's North Bailey, but by the time Boruwlaski met him he may have been living as a widower with his two unmarried daughters in a house on Claypath. The Count was immediately charmed by Ebdon, his daughters and the City of Durham.

The chances are that if Boruwlaski had first visited Durham around 1750, he might not have taken to it at all. The eighteenth century liked its landscapes to be rather tame, and enjoyed sparkling new buildings in the classical style. Joseph was not, however, too old to have absorbed the new romantic taste. The new generation relished wild, rugged places and crumbling, picturesque architecture. Boruwlaski describes Durham as 'romantic' in his 1820 autobiography, and as usual he hits the nail right on the head.

At Durham, a charitable gentleman called Smelt started to arrange a subscription for the Count. This might have raised enough money, from such people as the King and the Duke of Gloucester, to allow Boruwlaski to retire and settle down. Unfortunately the death of both Smelt and the Duke put paid to the scheme. The *Dictionary of National Biography* questions the chronology of these events, but in any case Boruwlaski found himself once again living by his wits.

He proceeded to Hull, and intended to go to America, like so many Polish exiles, but was prevented when the Misses Metcalfe, and various other friends both old and new, revived the subscription idea. This time, the scheme succeeded. Enough money was gathered together to enable the Count to buy an annuity and retire to Durham. According to Catherine Hutton's account in *Bentley's Miscellany*, Boruwlaski was already settled in Durham in 1807, and was able to 'keep house, and have a woman servant'. It may be that this 'keeping house' related to his living in a semi-independent way with his friend Thomas Ebdon and his daughters, Mary and Elizabeth.

5. Little Poland

In 1811 Thomas Ebdon died and the Count moved into Banks Cottage with the Misses Ebdon. This modest house, just outside the line of the old city walls, was leased to them for a peppercorn rent of two shillings a year, payable to the dean and chapter of the Cathedral. It is said that Boruwlaski referred to the cottage and its adjoining land as 'Little Poland'. A daughter of the Count's Durham friend James Raine remembered the house (now long gone) as small and inconvenient, but with a very wide mantle-piece in one of the rooms. This was where Boruwlaski's large servant was supposed to have put the Count when she was annoyed with him. Stranded in this position, the Count might have reflected that at least he wasn't on top of the cupboard, where his late wife used to put him.

Back home in Poland, in the spring of 1812, the people were enjoying the delicious sensation of hoping for liberty, which they thought would be theirs after Napoleon fought a war against Russia. Unfortunately, Napoleon's invasion of Russia started to unravel almost as soon as he crossed over into Russia from Poland. As winter set in, Bonaparte was facing a total disaster, and in 1814 he was forced to abdicate.

These events were celebrated in Durham by burning 'Boney' in effigy in the Market Place. If

Boruwlaski witnessed this, it must have been with mixed feelings. Yes, his adopted country had triumphed, but Russia now had the upper hand, and Poland's dream of freedom had come to nothing – for the time being.

The subject status of his native country may have convinced the Count that he really could not return. In effect, the huge, proud country that had given him birth hardly existed any more.

In 1820, Boruwlaski again published his autobiography by subscription – the first time he had done this since an Edinburgh edition in 1801. The 1820 autobiography is in English throughout, and the frontispiece consists of an engraving of the Count which is striking, unusual, and touching.

All the artists who depicted Joseph had to find a way to indicate that he was a little person. The frontispiece of the 1788 autobiography shows him *en famille*, so that the presence of his wife (and her huge hat) conveys the message that the man in the left of the picture is very small.

The 1792 frontispiece, and the painting by Reinagle, put Joseph up against pieces of regular-sized furniture. The 1820 engraving, by Downman after an original by Bouet, has the Count again posed with a person of average growth; in this case a young woman. But here we see neither of the subjects of the picture full-length, and the point of view of the artist is very low down – at about the level of Boruwlaski's chest.

This startling approach means that the artist can dispense with having to depict the floor, or rather the ground, as there are clouds in the background, suggesting an outdoor setting.

The young lady who is squeezed into the left of the engraving is slightly hunched over, as if in an unconscious attempt to reduce her height and get down to the Count's level. She is looking slightly away from the Count, as if embarrassed by one of his flirtatious remarks.

He looks slightly anxious, as if he has had to pause in the middle of a sentence to check its effect on the young lady. The index finger of his right hand is raised in a spirited way, as if the artist wanted to picture Boruwlaski's continental mode of gesticulating.

The Count must have been about eighty-one here, and at last he has abandoned his red military coat. He wears a dark cutaway jacket with an immaculate display of white linen between the widely-spaced lapels. The jacket looks a lot like the real one now displayed in the Durham Town Hall, and the one shown on his statue, and in the large painting by Hastings, also in the Town Hall.

The white wig has gone, along with the military coat, and the Count wears his hair loose, curly and combed forward, as does the young woman in the picture. The Count's eyes are large and shiny, and there seems to be the impression of spectacles on the bridge of his nose. Perhaps he wore reading-glasses.

Detail of statue in Durham Town Hall
© SW & Durham City Council

By 1820 the Count had lived in Durham for around a decade, and no doubt everybody in the genteel community had heard all his stories at least once. As a result, some new memories seem to have sprung up spontaneously in the mind of the Little Count, much as crocodiles were once thought to be born out of the fertile mud of the Nile. The Count no doubt felt obliged to put these new stories into the 1820 autobiography, since if they were not there the local friends who subscribed to the book would miss them. These tales include a meeting with the French philosopher Voltaire, and journeys to very remote and inhospitable places in Europe and beyond.

If Boruwlaski had really met Voltaire, he would surely have mentioned it in his 1788 autobiography, where he takes pleasure in dropping the names of many aristocrats and spirits of the age. Voltaire died in 1778, but in London in 1788 there might have been people who had known Voltaire, and could have sniffed out any fake stories about him. In Durham in 1820, there would probably have been very few, if any, people qualified to question Boruwlaski's Voltaire anecdote.

The Count's stories about such remote and inaccessible places as Kamchatka do contain some corroborating details, but we know that he owned at least one geography book, from which he might have cribbed a few useful facts.

In 1821 Boruwlaski went down to London to visit his old friend George IV, who had once been the Prince Regent. Even though this monarch was in the middle of preparations for his imminent coronation, he made time to see the Count, and his friend the comedian Charles Mathews.

This regal occasion is recorded in great detail in the biography of Mathews, written by his wife. The Count presented George with a copy of his 1820 autobiography, and George gave Joseph another watch, a fine gold one. This timepiece seems to have been an improvement on the 'pretty little' watch the Prince Regent had sent Boruwlaski years before.

According to Catherine Hutton, the watch was very small, with a 'delicate Trinchinopoly chain, and minute seals'.

George was keen to make sure his friend didn't want for anything financially, and he asked both the Count and Mathews about this, very earnestly. The King then enquired after Isalina, only to discover that she had been dead for thirty years. 'Fine woman! Sweet, beauty body!' the Count assured him.

Boruwlaski was permitted to view the clothes George was about to wear for his coronation. These included a ludicrous 'Spanish' hat with ostrich plumes and a giant train that had to be held up by nine men. The coronation robe alone cost £24,000 (over a million pounds today).

Charles Mathews, with whom Boruwlaski visited the new king, had started out as a comedy actor, but after 1808 toured Britain and America in his one-man show, called *At Home*, or *Mathews at Home*. This 'monopolylogue' seems to have been something like a complete evening at a music-hall, with songs, sketches and jokes, but all performed by the chameleon-like Mathews impersonating various characters.

Like Boruwlaski himself, Mathews was a good mimic, and he could 'do' the Little Count to a 'T'. Mathews made a point of making friends with foreigners, and he revelled in their strange accents and broken English.

Whenever he visited Durham, Mathews looked up his old friend, and wrote engaging letters back home about their time together. It is to Mathews that we owe an account of one of Boruwlaski's regular visits to the grocer from whom he bought the annuity on which he lived in his last years.

That such a financial product should have been bought from a grocer may seem strange, but we must remember that the availability of banking services for ordinary individuals was very limited at the time. Many people in various branches of business, who had accounts at local banks or at the

Bank of England, would 'sublet' banking services to others.

The Count was in his early seventies when he bought the annuity, and the grocer, it seems, did not think he would last much longer. Little did he know that the remarkable Pole would live over twenty-five years more, over which time the lump sum Boruwlaski had paid in exchange for his annuity would be completely exhausted. The Count's longevity meant that, in effect, the grocer and his heirs ended up paying the annuity out of their own pockets.

According to Mathews' biography, the Count enjoyed visiting the unfortunate grocer, who died long before he did. The book records the Count's comments after one such visit, in a way that preserves something of the Count's Polish accent and unusual English grammar:

'He fifty year yonger den Boruwlaski; mintime he dead sooner as me. Oh yes, you may be sure dat – dat is my oppinnon...Boruwlaski never die – you may depend.'

The Count called the grocer a 'poor hold body', and indeed it was his habit to use the word 'body' instead of 'person', 'man', 'woman', 'gentleman', etc. This he may have got from the Durham dialect, where phrases such as 'canny body' (meaning a reasonably good person) are common.

It may seem cruel of the Count to have mocked the grocer in this way, but Joseph was now his own man, and no longer needed to be polite to, or about, anyone.

In old age, Boruwlaski could also be very rude to

people's faces, on occasion. The occasions often had something to do with the fact that he could still be mistaken for a child, especially from the back, and in the 1820s and 30s adults were a lot less restrained about man-handling strange children than they are today.

Sometimes complete strangers would grab Joseph and put him in a chair, carry him over a puddle, or playfully pull his hair from the back. On these occasions, Boruwlaski would display his ability to swear 'like a Flemish trooper'. The exceptions to this happened if the person who had taken liberties with the Count turned out to be a good-looking woman. Then, the Count would be quite charming, and wouldn't swear at all.

When he was not being visited by his friend Charles Mathews, or staying with Mathews in London, Boruwlaski spent much of his time reading, writing and conducting chemical experiments. Some of his writing seems to have consisted of letters written to old friends, such as Catherine Hutton of Birmingham.

In one of these letters to Hutton, written in 1833, Boruwlaski included the little poem:

Poland was my cradle,
England is my nest;
Durham is my quiet place,
Where my weary bones shall rest.

It seems that Joseph's reading habits were by no means frivolous. Although his spoken English was eccentric to say the least, he owned an impressive collection of books in that language, and in French.

The catalogue of the items put up for auction after his death reveals that Boruwlaski owned the all-important Bible and *Complete Works* of Shakespeare, as well as '*Cook's Geography*', some books on chemistry, several volumes of Polish history in English, spare copies of his autobiographies and bound back-issues of both *The Saturday Magazine* and *The Gentleman's Magazine*.

As something of a health-nut, Joseph clearly understood that man cannot live by reading and writing alone. For exercise, he regularly walked round the banks of the river with his friend, the enormous actor Stephen Kemble, who at one time ran the theatre in Saddler Street, Durham. This unlikely pair were often to be seen in the bookshop of George Andrews, also in Saddler Street, which was then known as a 'literary rendezvous'. Andrews, whose premises remained a bookshop well into the twentieth century, was a publisher as well as a bookseller and stationer.

The Count was often invited out, for instance by the officials of the Cathedral, or by James Raine, the Rector of St Mary-the-Less in the South Bailey. Margaret Hunt, Raine's daughter, remembered seeing him at their home, Crook Hall, a picturesque old country house just outside the city.

Not having seen such a small adult before, she was confused as to exactly what he was, and why all the adults present treated him as another adult.

In his introduction to the Count's 1820 autobiography, which he edited, William Burdon comments on the Count's excellent playing, on both violin and guitar; and his tireless dancing. This suggests that, in those days when people 'made their own entertainment' the Count was quite happy to make some entertainment for his friends.

The 'Count's House' - © Miranda Brown

As well as Burdon, James Raine, George Andrews and Stephen Kemble, Boruwlaski's Durham friends may have included the architect Ignatius Bonomi. Bonomi, Raine and the Misses Ebdon signed the Little Count's probate document after his death, and Bonomi may have designed the Doric temple now known as the 'Count's House'. The building is too much of a text-book Greek Temple to have any telltale Bonomi features, but it does bear a striking resemblance to the lodge Bonomi designed for Windlestone Hall, near Durham.

North Lodge, Windlestone Hall © Oliver Dixon

Boruwlaski may also have been friends with the French-born drawing-master at Durham School, Nicholas Bouet, who did some charming informal portraits of the Count, and also of Bonomi.

Given his great age, his evident health and his habit of drinking no alcohol, it is not surprising that Boruwlaski should have been taken up as an example by one of the leading lights of the temperance movement. A Mr Harle, president of the Durham Temperance Society, used the example of Boruwlaski in a speech delivered in 1834. Here he revealed that the Count's diet consisted of little more than bread, coffee and puddings. By 'puddings' he would probably not have meant 'desserts' but proper old-fashioned British puddings, both sweet and savoury.

'Count' Joseph Boruwlaski died at home in Banks Cottage on September the fifth, 1837, of what was described in the London *Times* as 'a general decay of nature'. This was the year when an eighteen year-old girl called Victoria became Queen, and when Dickens finished the serialisation of his first novel *The Pickwick Papers*. It was also the year when the first railway station opened in London, Rowland Hill invented the postage stamp, and the first practical telegraph line was patented.

On the morning of Monday the eleventh of September, the Count was laid to rest under the flagstones of Durham Cathedral, where a stone inscribed with the letters 'JB' now marks the spot. The ceremony was strictly private. A black marble memorial plaque was made to go on a wall nearby, but this has ended up in the church of St Mary-the-Less in South Bailey, where Joseph's friend James Raine was Rector.

Violin, chair, shoes, slippers and top hat case
at Durham Town Hall
© SW & Durham City Council

Boruwlaski died intestate, and his probate record shows that the Misses Ebdon were appointed as his executrices. The possessions auctioned in 1838 included a telescope, chemistry equipment, various small pieces of furniture, his violin and guitar, as well as a very respectable collection of books.

The University was a keen bidder at the auction of the Count's effects, and the items now displayed in the Town Hall were once at the Museum (now long closed) on Palace Green.

The portrait in oils by E. Hastings was raffled off, and now hangs in the Town Hall in Durham. This shows the Count with thinning, white hair.

On a table behind him rests his guitar, and on the small table to his left are his top-hat with a pair of white kid gloves draped over it, in the style of an English gentleman.

Given Boruwlaski's great age at death, we are bound to ask, what was his secret? Joseph's chronic good health might have had something to do with his habit of drinking only water and coffee, but in many of the places he visited he would have risked cholera by drinking water that had not been previously boiled. This would have been very much the case in cities, especially in the hot months of the year. And much of the water would have passed through lead pipes to get to the Count's glass.

Boruwlaski's diet of bread and puddings doesn't sound particularly healthy: one wonders how much in the way of fresh fruit and vegetables could have made it into those puddings.

Some say that a happy temperament and positive attitude can bring on long life, but, although he was often jolly in company, Joseph's way of life meant that he was also frequently both stressed and depressed.

He was very active, constantly travelling and promoting himself, until his early seventies, but then he enjoyed nearly thirty years of retirement, when he wasn't really obliged to do anything.

He did, of course, tell his friend Charles Mathews that he would live forever, and would continue to grow for hundreds of years. Perhaps, as some may have suspected during his life, his devotion to the pseudo-science of alchemy had something to do with it.

Hat-case, gloves and ring at Durham Town Hall
© SW & Durham City Council

6. Epilogue in Narnia

Long after Boruwlaski's death, the English writer C.S. Lewis noticed a lamp-post apparently lost in the woods by Prebends Bridge in Durham.

This strange sight, which is still to be seen in that place, contributed to Lewis's ideas for a novel where a group of children discover a wood, and a lamp-post, inside a wardrobe.

Prebends Bridge is very near the Count's House, and one cannot help wondering if the classical architecture of the temple fed into Lewis's use of mythological creatures such as fauns and centaurs in his Narnia novels.

When Edmund stumbles into Narnia, he encounters the terrifying White Witch, whose sledge is driven by a little person who is about three feet high.

© Miranda Brown

Further Reading:

Boruwlaski, Joseph: *Memoirs*, London, 1788
Boruwlaski, Joseph: *Memoirs*, J. Thompson, 1792
Boruwlaski, Joseph: *Memoirs*, Francis Humble, 1820
Crosby, J.H.: *Ignatius Bonomi of Durham; architect*, City of Durham Trust, 1987
Heron, Tom: *Boruwlaski: The Little Count*, City of Durham, 1986
Leroi, Armand Marie: *Mutants*, Harper Collins, 2003
Lewis, C.S.: *The lion, the witch and the wardrobe*, Diamond Books, 1998
Mickiewicz, Adam: *Pan Tadeusz*, Everyman, 1966
Pevsner, Nikolaus: *The buildings of England: County Durham*, second edition revised by Elizabeth Williamson, Penguin, 1985
Prazmowska, Anita J.: *A history of Poland*, Palgrave, 2004
Zamoyski, Adam: *The last King of Poland,* Weidenfeld & Nicolson, 1992

For free downloads and more from the Langley Press, please visit our website at:

http://tinyurl.com/lpdirect

Printed in Poland
by Amazon Fulfillment
Poland Sp. z o.o., Wrocław